HOW TO CREATE EXCITING

ART AND CRAFT ACTIVITIES FOR CHILDREN

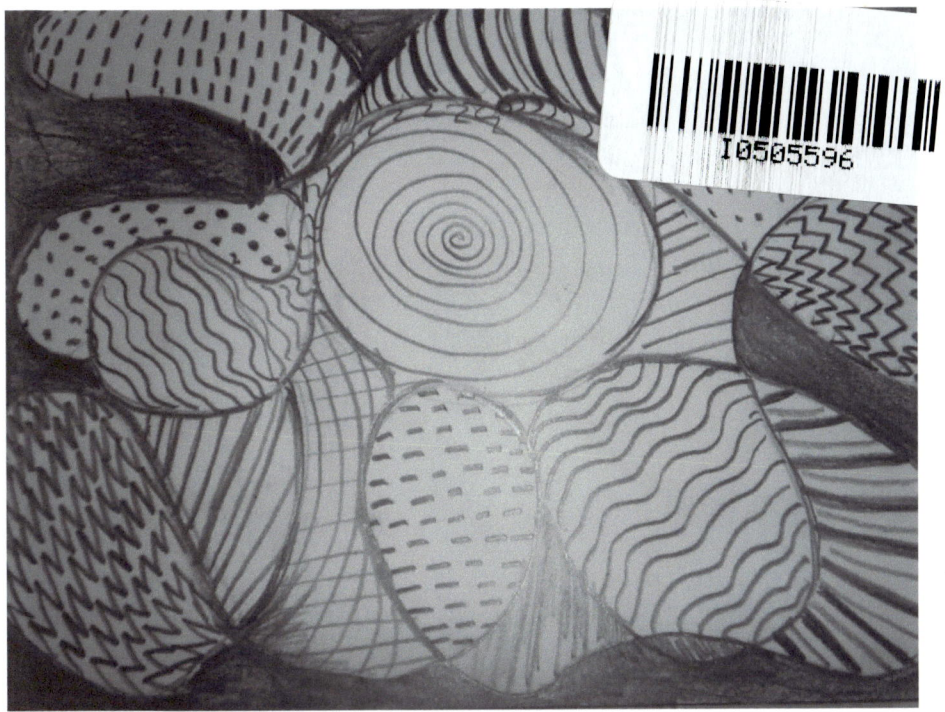

I0505596

How to Draw Series

Evadne Taylor

Mendon Cottage Books

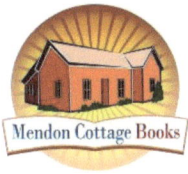

JD-Biz Publishing

All Rights Reserved.

No part of this publication may be reproduced in any form or by any means, including scanning, photocopying, or otherwise without prior written permission from JD-Biz Corp Copyright © 2015

All Images Licensed by Fotolia and 123RF.

Our books are available at

1. Amazon.com

2. Barnes and Noble

3. Itunes

4. Kobo

5. Smashwords

6. Google Play Books

Table of Contents

Introduction

Visual Art is one avenue where people of every race and creed can express themselves. Children, in particular, tend to crave this vehicle of expression as they go through the artistic stages: scribbling, pre-schematic, schematic, and visual realism. Each stage is vital to the child's development, and artistic expression should be encouraged as much as possible. Parents and teachers sometimes stifle this creative side of children by not providing opportunities for artistic expression. It is sometimes due to their lack of knowledge or fear of the subject.

This book will highlight ten art topics that can be used at home or in the classroom to encourage artistic expressions and spark creativity in children and interested adults.

Chapter 1 – Crayon Resist

Crayon resist is a type of artwork that is ideal for children and adults who want to create something interesting.

This technique involves the use of crayon and watercolor paint combined. As the word suggests, the crayon resists the paint and creates a batik-like effect on the surface.

Materials needed

- An 8x10 piece of cartridge paper

- Pencil

- Wax crayons

- Watercolor paint (one color per work)

- Scissors

- 1paintbrush

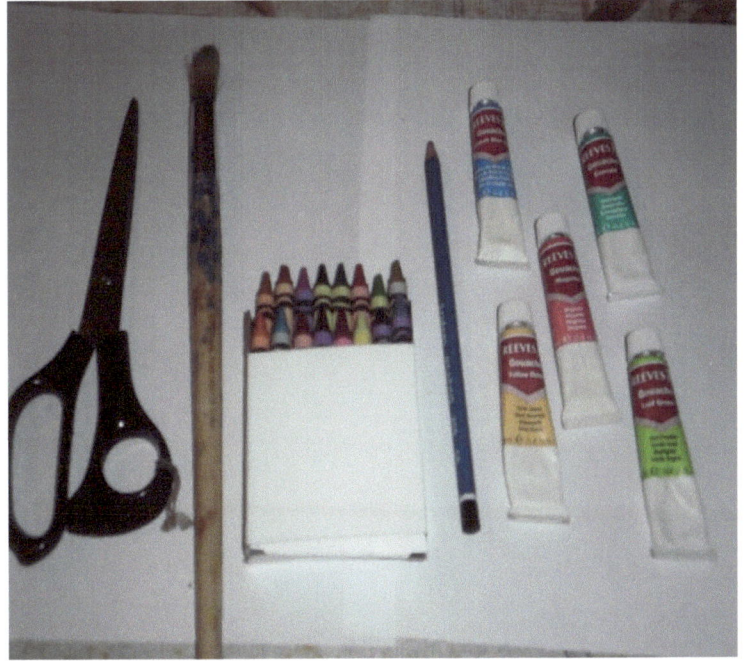

Technique

1. Cut a piece of cartridge paper measuring 8x10

2. Use the pencil to draw something of your choice – an animal, an underwater scene, a flower, a butterfly, etc.

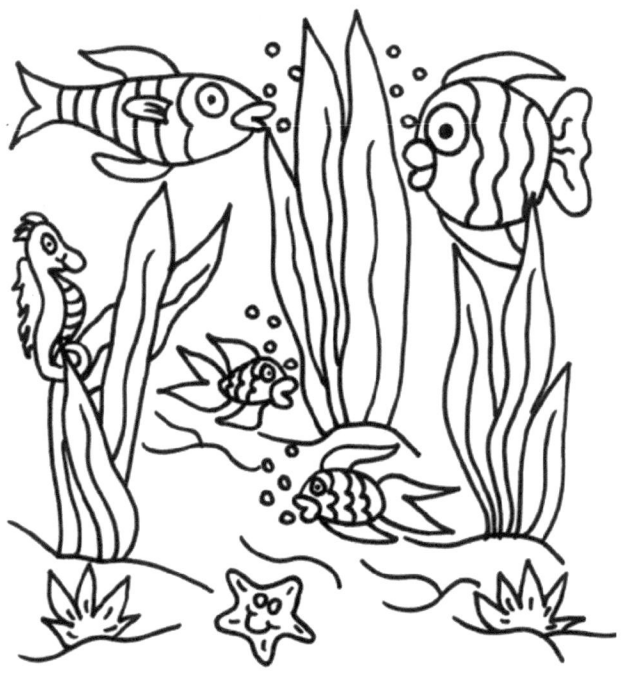

3. Use the crayon to color your picture. The crayons must be used heavily, with the artist pressing down on them as hard as possible. Take note that the white crayons may also be used as this will be highlighted when the paint goes on.

4. When all areas are covered with the wax crayon, set the work aside for a while.

5. Prepare a cup or pallet with watercolor paint.

6. Retrieve the artwork and use the brush to apply the paint all over the surface of the paper – especially over the crayoned areas.

7. Allow it to dry thoroughly.

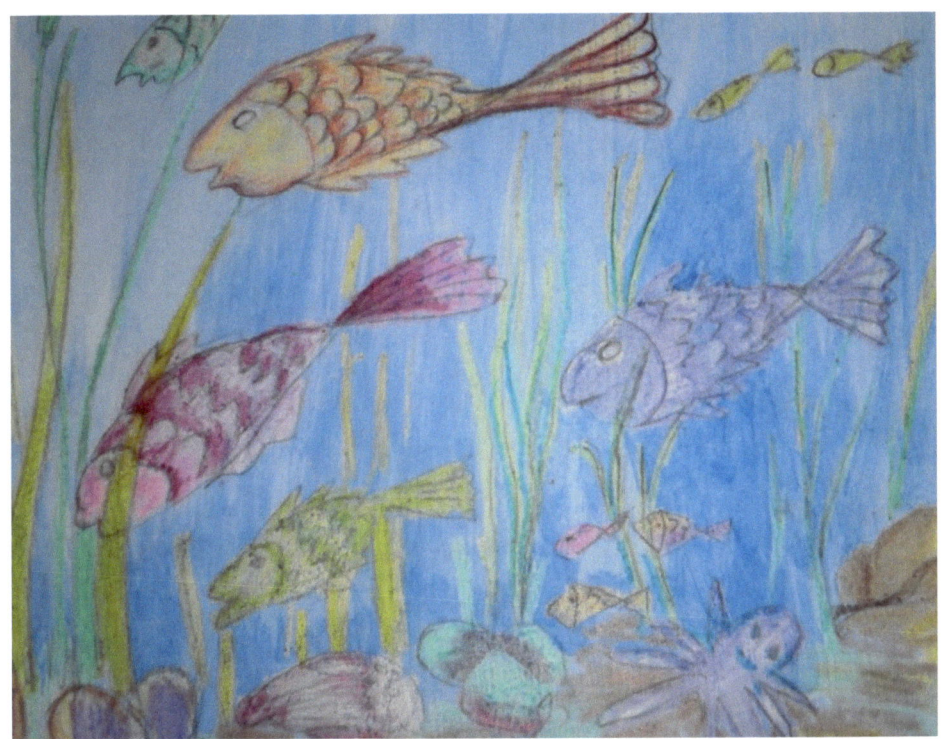

Evadne Taylor. Underwater scene, Crayon etching

Chapter 2 - Printmaking

A print is a mark that is made when paint or ink is put on an object or a surface and pressure is applied as the image is stamped onto another surface to make a print.

Printmaking started from as early as 150 AD in China. They used rice paper to draw the designs and transferred them onto a woodblock. They then used the wood to make prints.

Many types of printing exist, and are used to enhance a wide range of surfaces. Prints are used for decorative purposes, as well as for advertising. Some types of prints are:

Lino Prints: Lino prints are made from inked Lino blocks, parts of which have been cut away.

Screen printing: A silk screen is used for this method. A piece of very thin fabric, called an organza, is stretched on a rectangular frame. A previously cut stencil is placed on the back of the screen and the print is made as the ink is dispersed into the open screen using a squeegee.

Etching: This involves copper or zinc sheets, in which acid is used to chemically remove layers to produce a picture.

Lithography: This is usually an image made on a flat surface, such as an aluminum plate, that is then transferred to a flexible sheet. An oil-based ink is applied to the plate and then a piece of paper is placed over the plate.

Block printing: A design is carved out on the surface of a block of wood, which is then inked and printed on another surface.

Mono prints: A mono print is a single print. A slightly raised surface is inked with one color and then printed on a surface.

Stencil printing: In stenciling a design is cut out of the stencil leaving the negative spaces which are to be printed. Ink is then applied to these negative spaces with an applicator to make a print on any given surface.

Chapter 3 - Mono printing using Styrofoam meat trays

Materials needed:

- 8"x10" cartridge paper

- Clean meat trays

- Ink or acrylic paint

- A blunt tool for carving

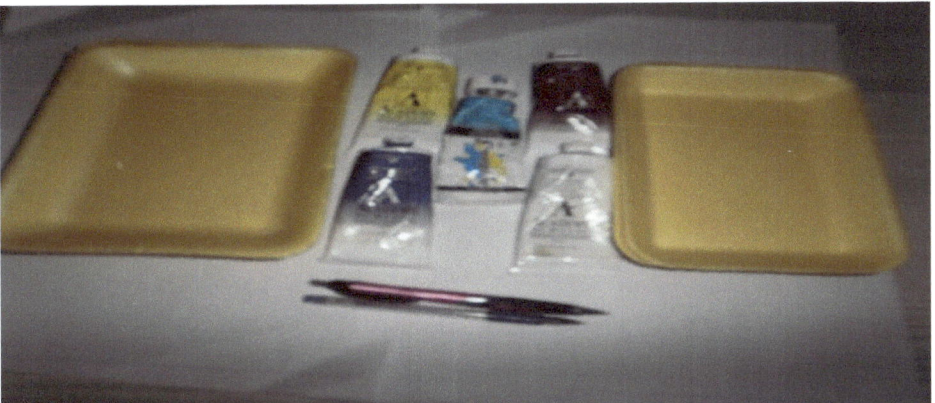

Technique

Thoroughly wash and dry a Styrofoam meat tray. Cut the sides of the tray so that the tray is flat.

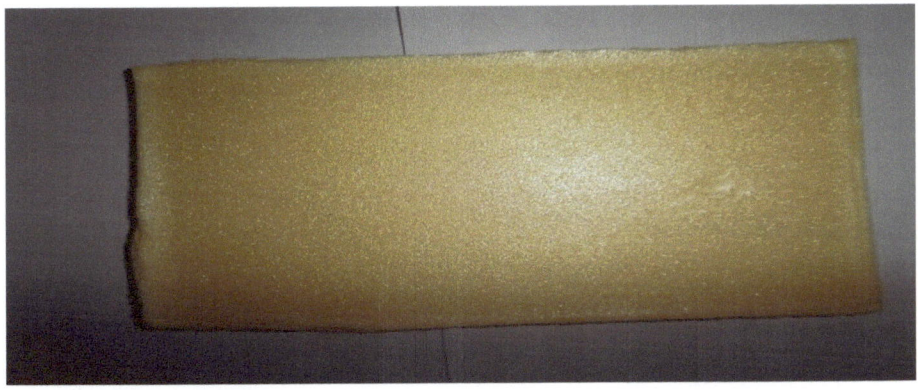

Sketch a design on a piece of paper and transfer it to the Styrofoam later. If you are confident enough, you may draw your design directly onto the Styrofoam.

Etch design onto the Styrofoam, creating some raised areas.

With a medium sized paint brush, paint the surface of the meat tray with a bit of acrylic paint covering all areas.

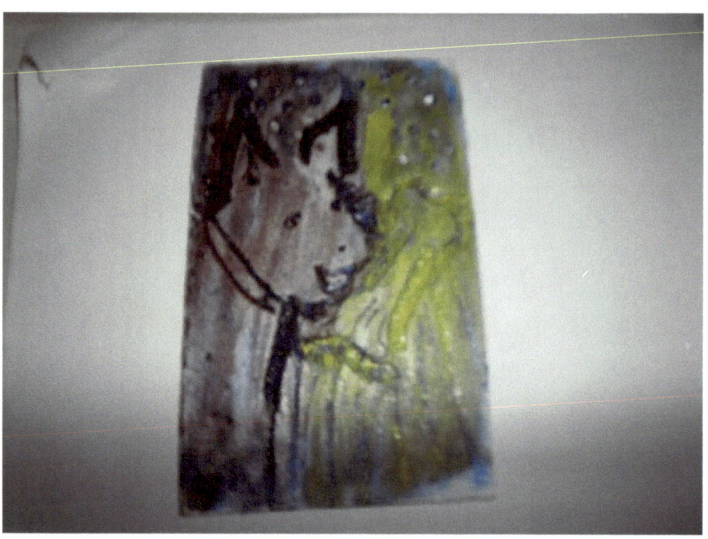

The Styrofoam is etched and then painted

Select the area on the paper where you would like to place the print and press it firmly onto the surface.

When the impression has been made, carefully remove the paper from the Styrofoam to reveal the print.

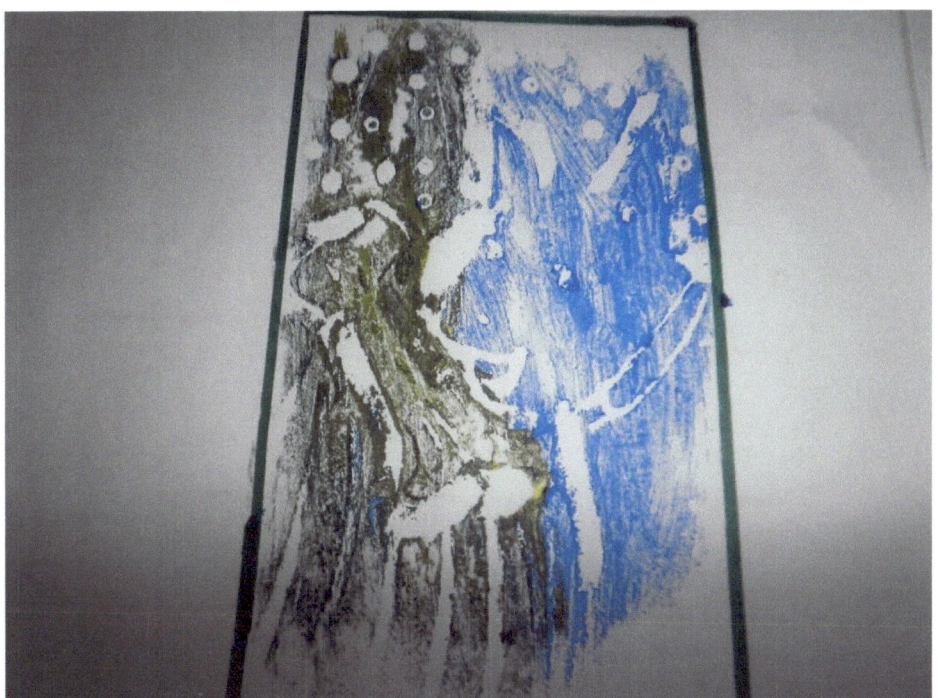

Evadne Taylor - 'Catching a Bone'

Chapter 4 - Leaf printing

Leaves are found in many artistic designs. They have been used by numerous artists to create aesthetically pleasing art pieces, or to decorate a myriad number of surfaces. Leaves are found in nature and are therefore categorized as organic shapes. Organic shapes are irregular shapes, primarily found in nature. They have no specific measurement or rigid straight edges. Another type of shape that is somewhat opposite to the organic shape is the geometric shape. You will learn more about this shape in subsequent activities.

I will be exploring two techniques to leaf printing: leaf printing using paint, and leaf printing using crayons.

Using crayons

For this project you will need:

- Beautifully- shaped leaves

- Paper

- Crayons

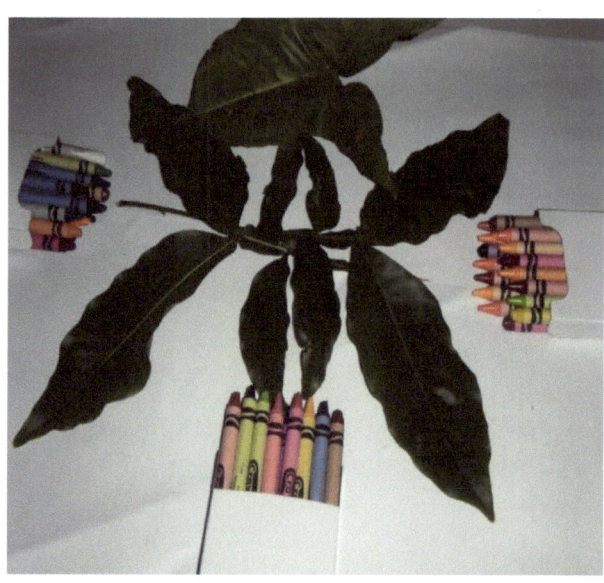

Technique

Select 5 to 6 leaves of the same shape and arrange them on a table in the same way that you would like your final design to look. Ensure that they are placed firmly on the surface. Also, the back of the leaves should be turned upwards so that the veins will help to leave a better impression on the paper.

Use a clean white paper and place it over the arranged leaves. Use a small bit of tape on the four corners of the paper to secure it onto the surface and on to the leaves.

Select the crayons that you would like to work with. It would be best to stick with two to three colors. Feel for the edges of the leaves and begin coloring each shape that is felt. Work through the design until all the impressions of the leaves are visible.

Remove your paper from the leaves and examine your work. The negative spaces, or those areas without any leaf marks, may be colored using another color from the chosen color scheme.

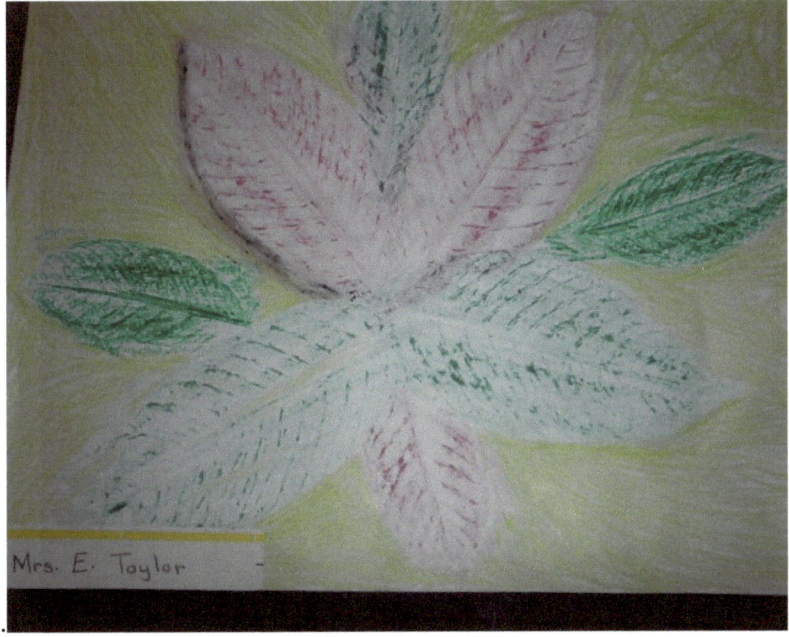

Mrs. E. Taylor

Leaf printing using paint

For this technique you will need:

- 1 piece of white cartridge paper (8x10)

- Poster paint

- 1 paint brush

- Leaves with interesting shapes

Technique

Before you begin, decide how you want to arrange your work and what color scheme you would like to use.

Color schemes are a harmonious combination of colors. These schemes fall under three major groups: related colors, contrasting colors, and neutrals.

Related colors are based on shades of the same color, e.g.: Shades of red or shades of purple.

Contrasting colors are unrelated colors that are usually positioned on the opposite sides of the color wheel.

Complementary colors are one example of contrasting colors. The complementary color for red is green, the complementary color for blue is orange, and the complementary color for yellow is purple.

For this leaf printing project I will choose to use the complementary colors yellow and purple.

Cover the paper with a shade of yellow. Apply a shade of purple paint on the side of the leaf that has the more pronounced veins. Having decided on the design for your space, press the leaf on the surface of the paper. You may use various shades of purple within the printed space. Work through your design until finished. Allow the work to dry thoroughly.

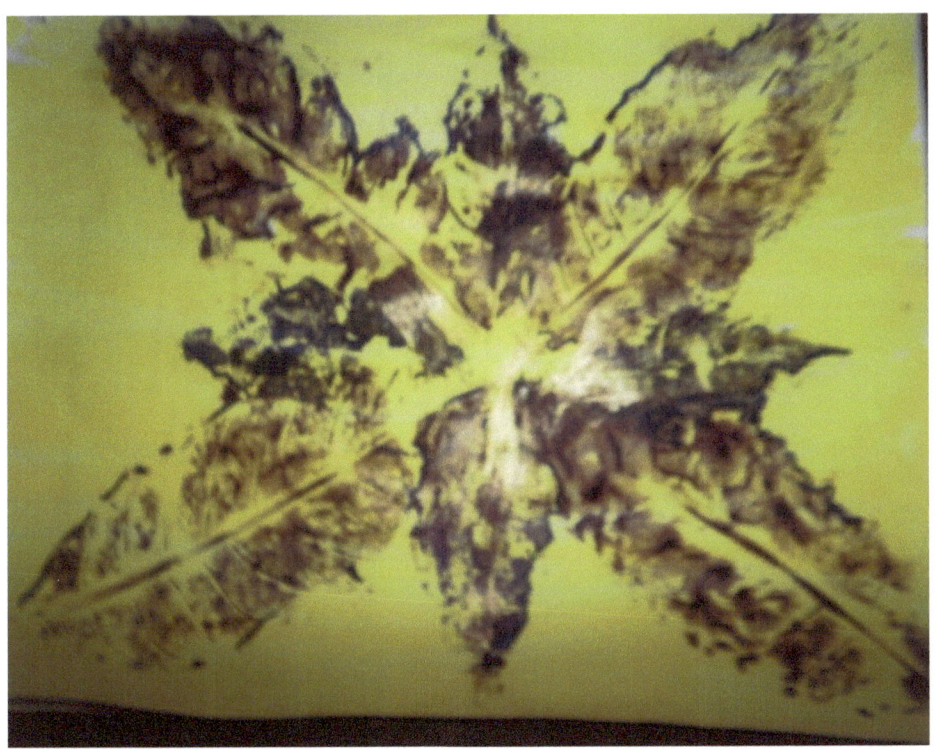

Leaf printing using paint

Chapter 5 - Stenciling

Stenciling is the art of cutting away a part of a design to allow ink or paint to go through, in order to create a print onto a surface. Stenciling is generally used to create borders on walls, floors, or furniture. It may be used to decorate any given surface, and can give the surface area a beautiful finish.

Stenciling was created in China in the eighth century AD. Stenciling can be either simple or complicated. In a complicated design, four or five colors may be used at a time.

For this project a simple design will be used.

Materials needed:

- Paper for stencil (typing paper may be used)

- Printing paper (cartridge paper may be used)

- Paint

- Scissors

- Sponge

Method

A simple stencil design may be created by folding the typing paper in quarters (in four). Use the scissors to cut out irregular shapes – as many as is needed.

Open the paper to reveal the shapes.

Ensure that the work surface is covered with newspaper. Place the cut stencil on top of the clean sheet of paper.

Use a clean sponge to pick up a bit of paint and gently apply it to the opened spaces of the stencil. Be sure that the paint is spread evenly on the surface of the sponge. Make sure that paint is applied to all the blank spaces in the design.

When that is completed, gently lift the stencil to reveal the printed design.

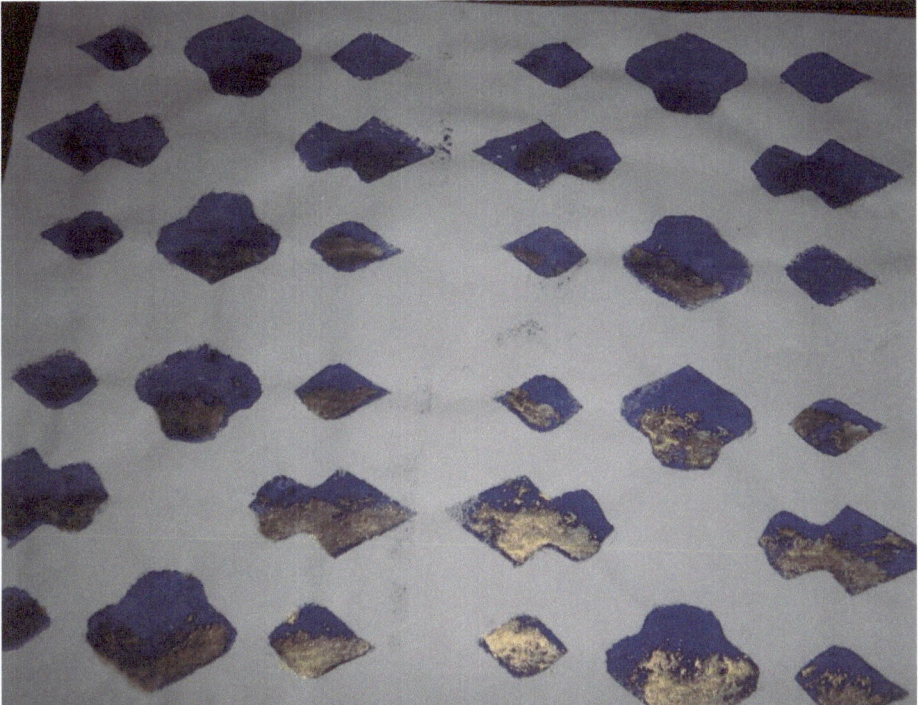

Stenciling using paint, Gold paint was used with the purple.

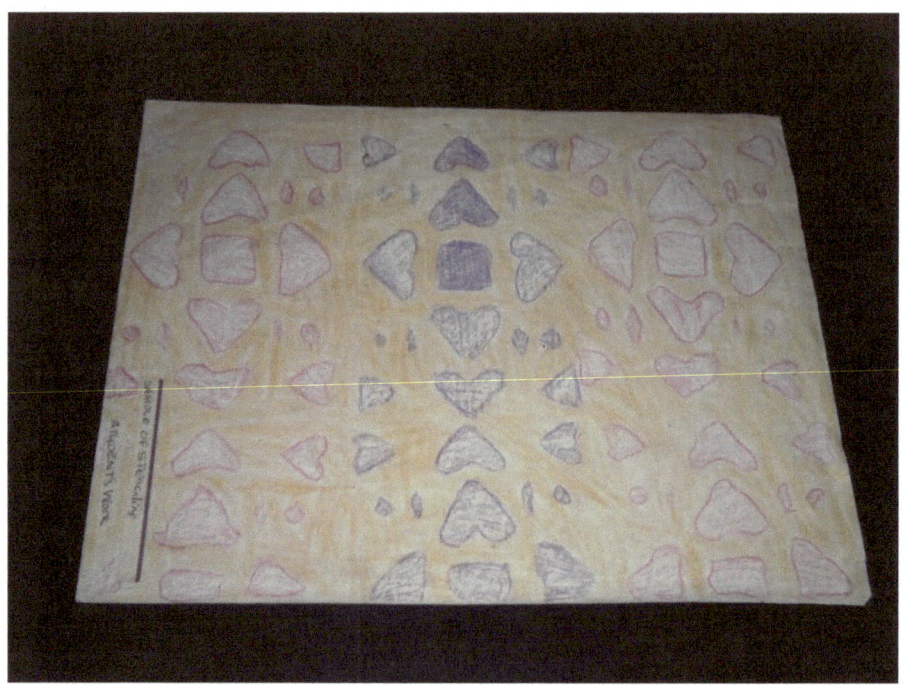

Stenciling, using pencil crayons.

When using the crayons, the stenciling becomes less messy and more controlled. The paper is cut in the same way and placed over the surface to be printed. The crayon is then used in the cut spaces and patiently worked until all spaces are colored. The background or negative spaces are then carefully colored in a chosen hue.

Chapter 6 - Exploring Line Designs

Lines are the most integral element of a design. In fact, there is no design without lines. A line is a path traced by a moving point. Every line has direction, thickness, and rhythm. Lines are found in every aspect of our environment. Just think of the vertical lines in the cane plant, the lines on the zebra, the train line, the light posts, your clothes, even the clothes you are wearing have lines.

There are many types of lines. Some of them are:

1. Vertical lines

2. Horizontal lines

3. Wavy lines

4. Broken lines

5. Dotted lines

6. Diagonal lines

Line Quality

Line quality refers to the special character of each line, whether it is a thick line, a thin line, a rough line, or a smooth line.

Combinations of these lines may be used to create dynamic works of art.

To create this line drawing you will need:

- An 8"x10" cartridge paper or construction paper.

- A writing tool – a pencil, a pen, colored pencils, or fine tipped markers.

Technique

You may begin by 'taking a line for a walk', that is, place the pencil at a point on the paper, and allow your hand to move all around the paper creating loops. This is also called 'trail- a- line'.

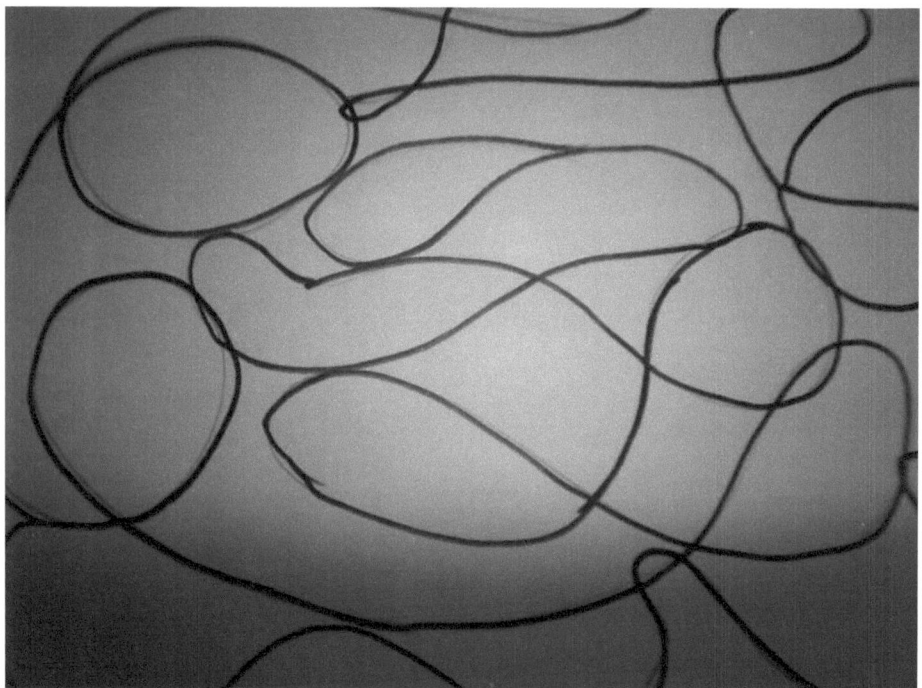

Ensure that the entire paper is filled with the lines.

Upon completion, fill each loop with a different type of line. Ensure that lines of various thickness and shades are used. Keep filling each loop until all the loops are filled.

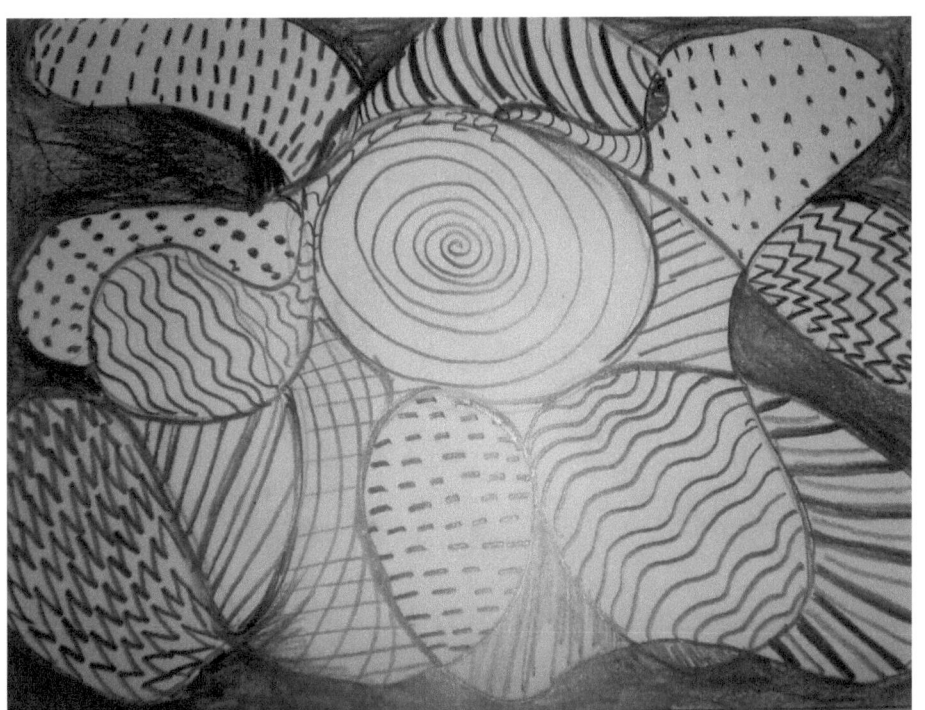

Chapter 7 – Wall Hanging using Discarded Tissue Roll

There are many things that may be done using discarded materials. Creating useful objects from everyday things that are thrown away can be beneficial in saving the environment.

Discarded bottle caps, bottles, paper plates, tissue rolls, and juice boxes are just a few of the myriad of things that may be used to create amazing, useful, and decorative items. People have used tires to create bags, belts, shoes, and other useful and wearable things.

Tissue roll is the cylindrical cardboard roll that holds the paper towel or toilet tissue in place before and during use. It is one of the most accessible materials, as millions of these rolls are discarded daily. It comes in various sizes and lends itself to be used in a wide range of creative expressions.

Tissue rolls can be used to make pencil and pen holders, desk organizers, decorative wall hangings, bracelets, Christmas ornaments and animal sculptures.

A decorative wall hanging will be made using tissue rolls cut in rings.

Materials:

For this project you will need:

- tissue rolls (as many as possible collected over time)

- glue

- spray paint or acrylic paint

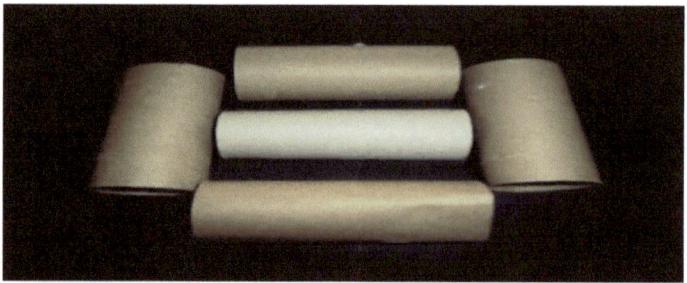

Technique:

Cut tissue rolls into rings, approximately four per roll.

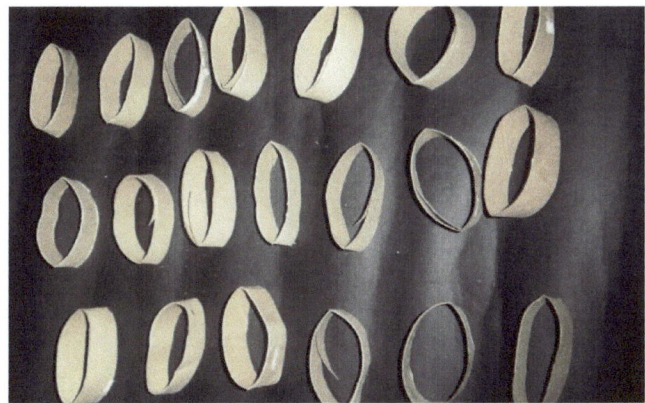

Use four such rings to make a four petal flower.

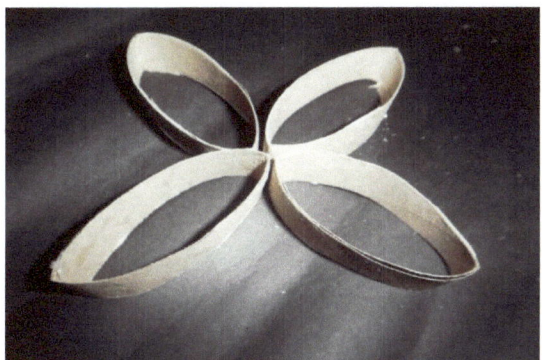

Build on the basic flower by adding a ring between the points of the flower

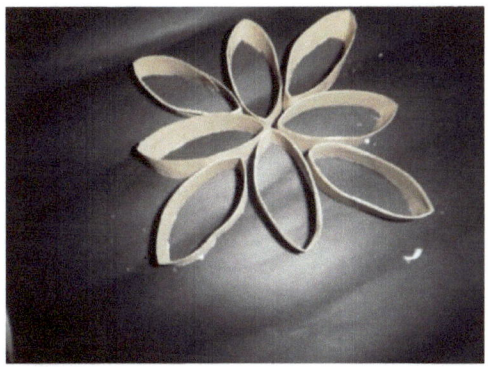

Keep building until the desired size is reached.

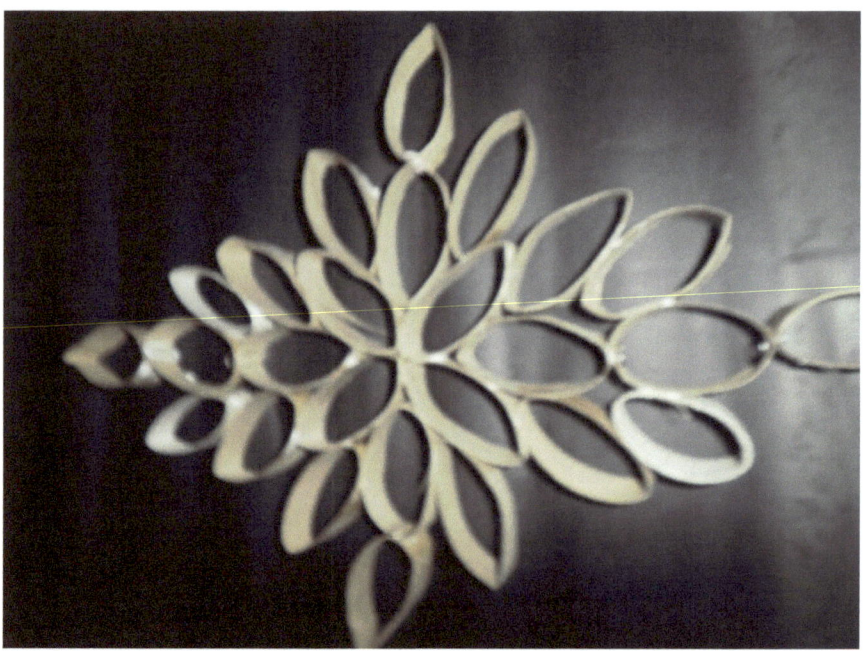

Decide on a color or colors and use spray paint or acrylic paint to give a beautiful finish.

Chapter 8 - Designs using shapes

Shapes are all around us. As was mentioned before, there are two types of shapes: geometric shapes and organic shapes. Organic shapes are found mainly in nature while geometric shapes are mathematical shapes such as triangles, squares, rectangles, etc. Many artists have worked with these shapes to execute dynamic works of art. One artist who used geometric shapes in his work is Pablo Picasso. He actually developed an art form called Cubism.

Pablo Picasso, born 1881, was a Spanish painter, sculptor, printmaker, and ceramist. He was one of the most original and prolific artist of the twentieth century. He was the co-founder of the art form called Cubism. Picasso used primarily geometric shapes to create his art work.

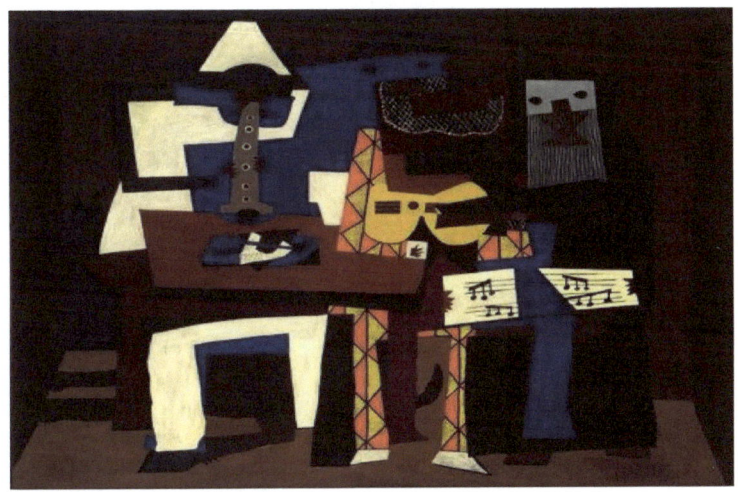

'Three Musicians' – Pablo Picasso

To create our own work using geometric shapes we will need:

1.   cartridge paper (8"x10")

2.   glue

3.   construction papers of various colors

4.   markers

5. scissors

Method

Use the scissors to cut various geometric shapes from the construction papers. Ensure that each shape is cut in many sizes.

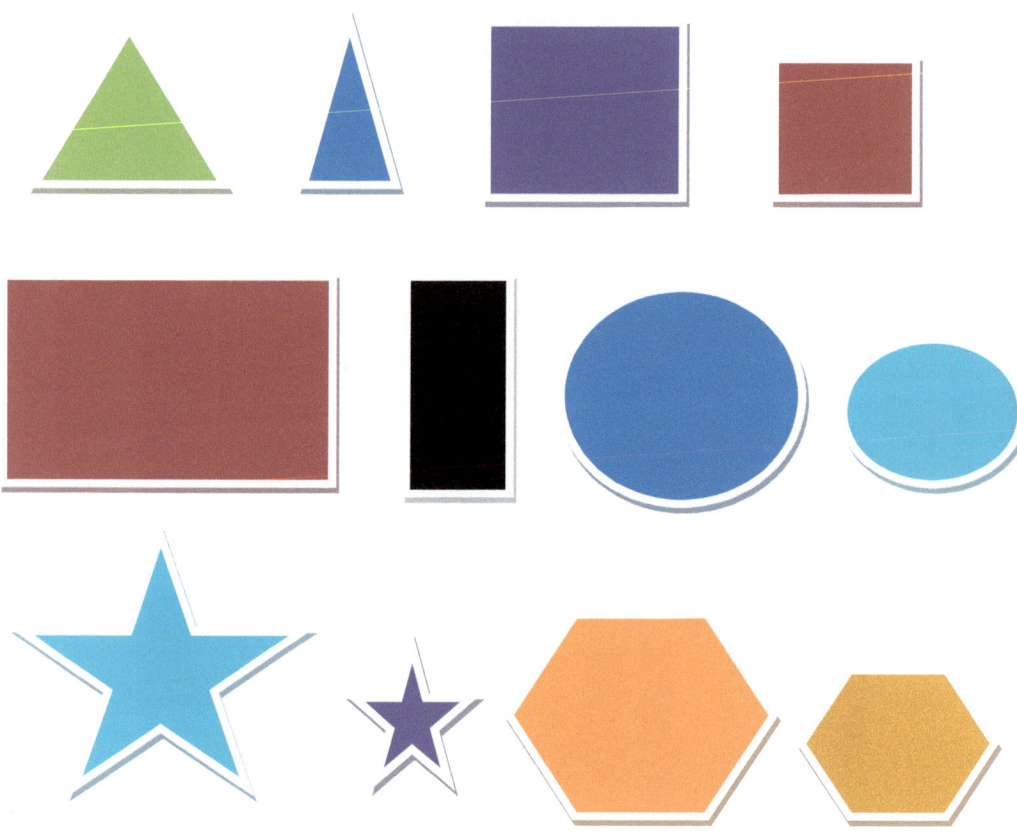

Decide on the design by placing several shapes of various sizes on the surface. Twist, turn, and adjust until the desired design is achieved. The shapes may overlap and one shape may be repeated numerous times depending on what is required.

Carefully glue each shape onto the surface until finished.

You may border the shapes with a marker.

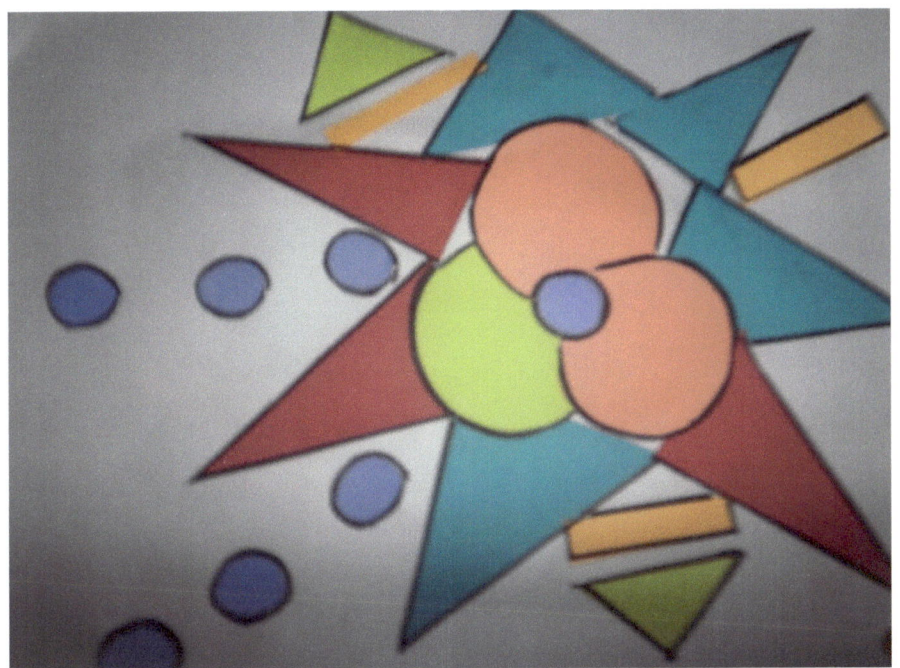

Another way to experiment with shapes is to actually draw the shapes on a piece of paper. Draw different geometric shapes, overlapping and repeating them in various sizes. When the desired design is achieved you may experiment with lines within the shapes themselves. Horizontal lines, zigzag lines, wavy lines, etc. may all be used within the design. Outline the design when completed.

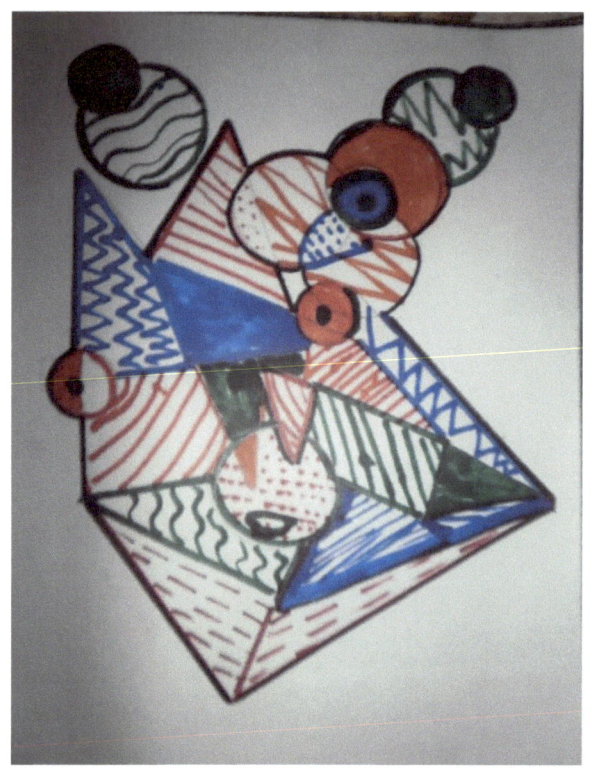

If desired, one could use color instead to complete the art work.

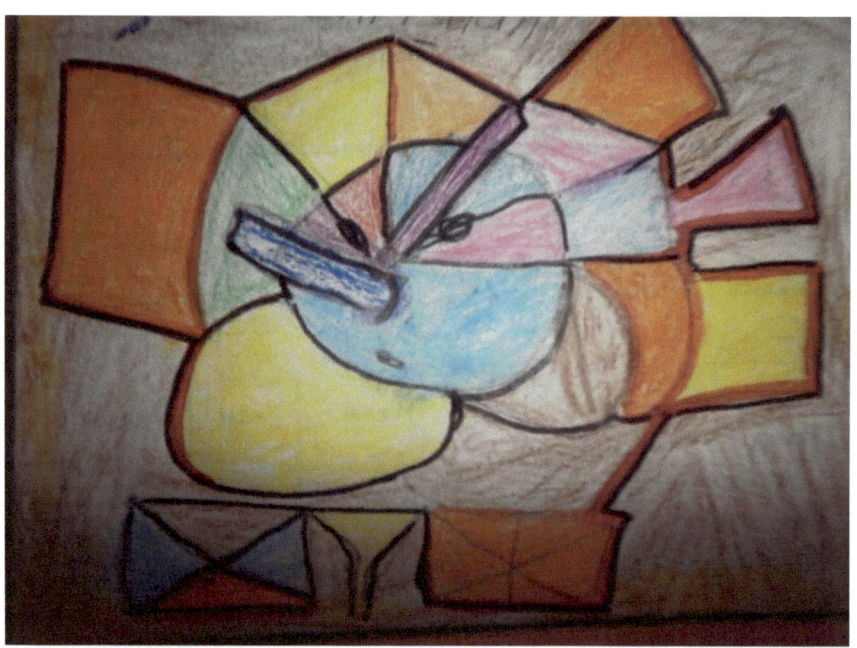

Chapter 9 - Tie and Dye

The technique of tie-dyeing is one of a wide range of cloth decorating and cloth dyeing techniques which began in ancient Egypt and Mesopotamia. Tie and dye technique initially spread from ancient Egypt to India, Greece, and Rome.

The method of tie and dye creates patterns on cloth by keeping some parts of the cloth free from the dye. Tie and dye is also known as 'resist- dyeing' and it involves tying the fabric in order to prevent the dye from penetrating through the tied areas and thus dying the untied areas. Tying is very important. The cloth must be bunched up so closely that the dye cannot reach the inside of the sample. If the bundle is loose the dye will soak through and the pattern will be lost.

The fabric is washed out before the dye is applied to eliminate any manufacturer's chemical that would prevent the dye from penetrating the fabric effectively.

Materials needed:

- Cotton fabric / T-shirts

- Various packs of dyes – multiple colors

- Bath tub or basin for dyeing

- Scissors

- Rubber bands

- Spoons or sticks for stirring the dye

- Overall or apron

- Measuring spoon

- Salt and or vinegar

- Iron

Tying methods

There are several tying methods which may be employed to achieve many types of print. When tying use the elastic bands to tie the fabric firmly so that no dye can penetrate the bounded areas.

- **Pleating** – this is created by accordion pleating the fabric and tying it at intervals along the fabric.

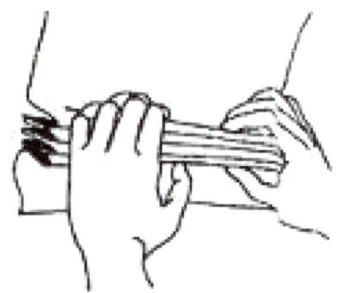

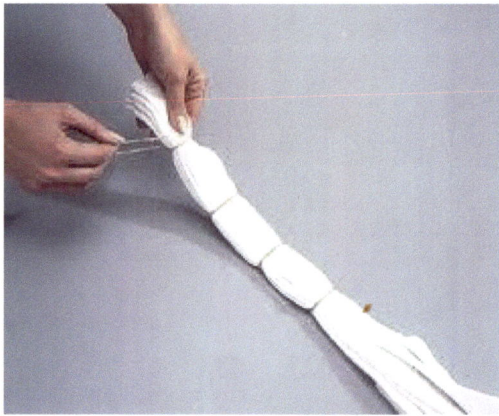

- **Marbling** – The material is rolled into a ball and tied all over.

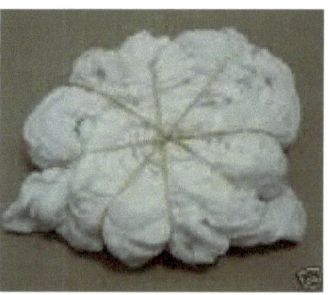

- **Circles** – Circles may be created by placing objects in the fabric and tying it.

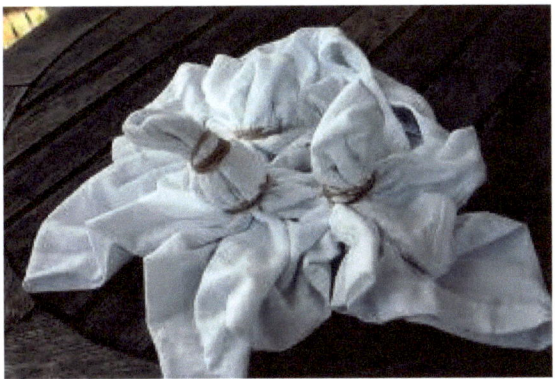

- **Sunburst** – The fabric is gathered from the center and tied in equal intervals.

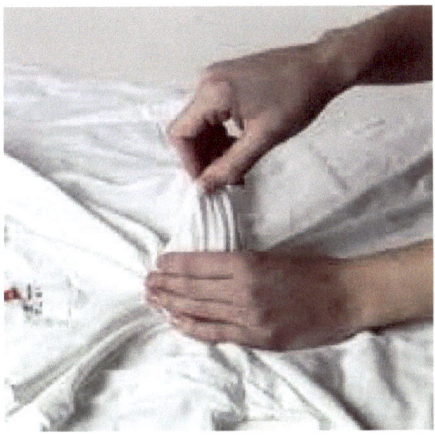

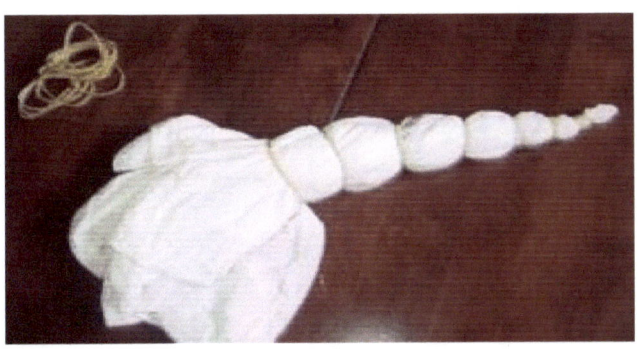

- **Squares** – Squares of the fabric are folded into quarters and then tied in places.

- **Triangles** – The square fabric is folded into quarters and then across in half to form a triangle.

- **Roughing** – The string is placed at the top of the fabric and the fabric is loosely rolled over the string. At the end of the rolling the string is drawn and tied.

The dye bath

Any vessel of enamel, stainless steel, and galvanized ware are suitable for hot and cold dyes. Besides these, for cold dyes only any containers which will not rust, made of glass or plastic can be used.

Bring water to a boil. Empty a pack of dye into a separate, smaller container and pour hot water into the container. Use a mixing stick and stir thoroughly until the dye is dissolved. 1tablespoon Vinegar and or salt must be added to the dye bath in order to stabilize it.

Pour into the larger dye bath and add cold water, enough to cover the fabric.

Before dyeing your tied-up sample, soak it in clean cold water for a moment. Take it out and squeeze it, or let it drain on newspaper before putting it in the dye.

Submerge material to be dyed into the dye bath. Use the stick to stir periodically. Allow the fabric to remain in the dye bath for about 30 minutes or until the desired shade of color is reached.

Remove from dye bath and rinse under cold water. Pull the tied areas to reveal the design and put to dry.

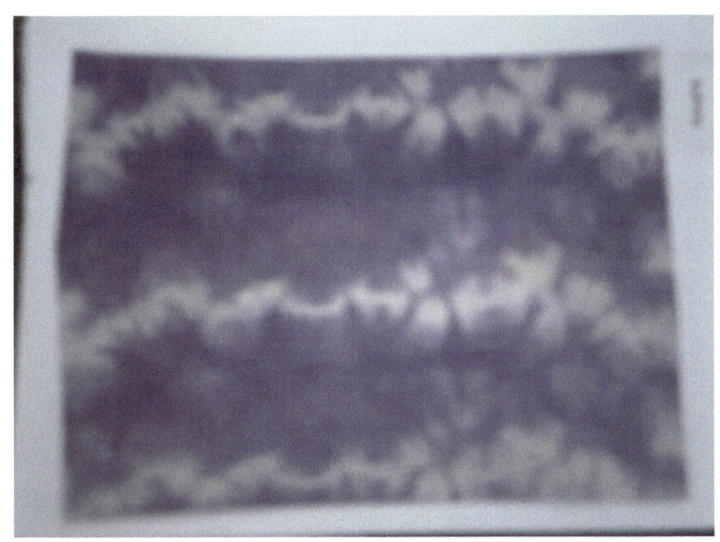

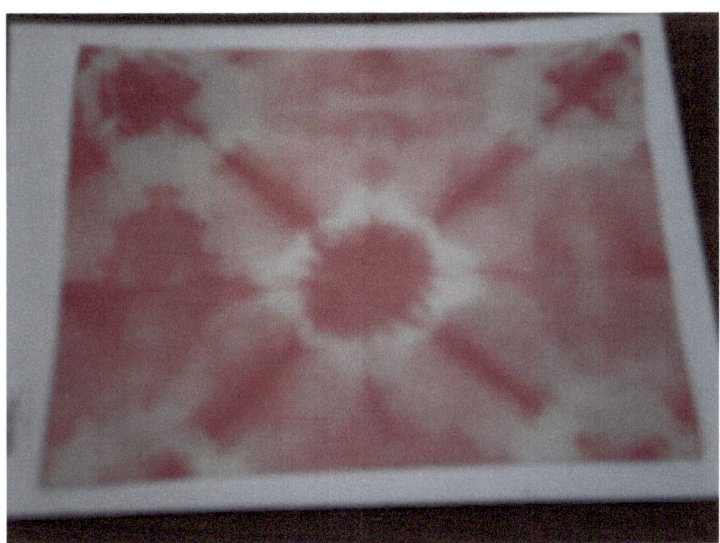

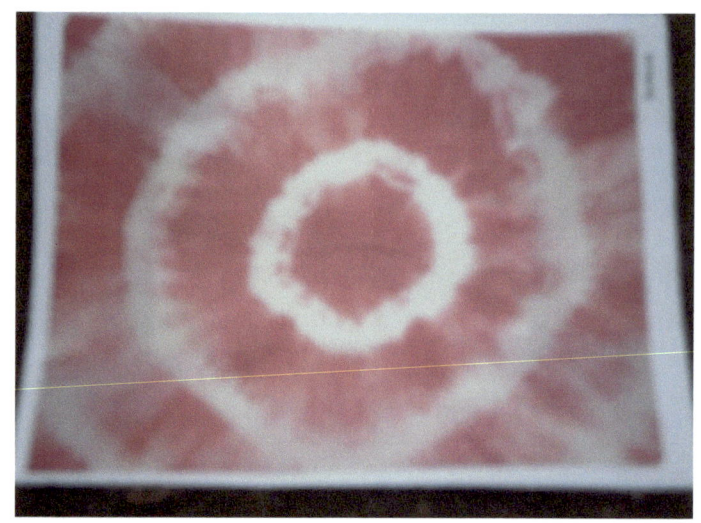

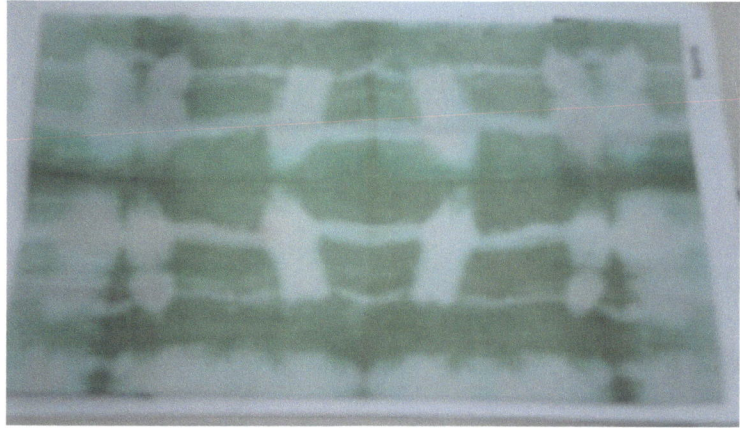

Chapter 10 - Mask Making

Masks are face coverings designed to hide someone's identity or for decoration. The art of mask making is more than 3,000 years old. The Egyptian tomb of King Tutankhamen was discovered by archeologists who found that the King's stunning mask was well preserved after many years. It was made of gold and a blue stone called lapis lazuli.

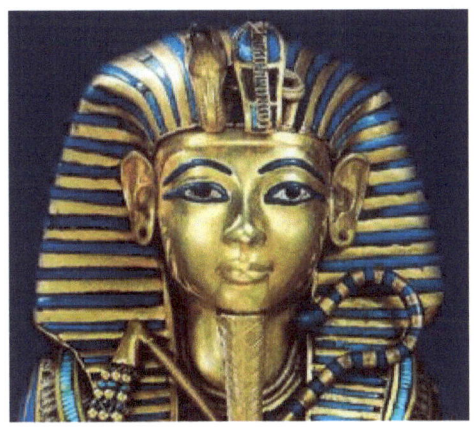

Masks have been a main feature of many festive activities including carnivals and Halloween parties. Masks are also worn by many actors and actresses in theatres, at football matches, and other games where mascots are decked out in masks and other costumes. Thieves also use masks to conceal their identities as they execute their devious activities.

Masks are shown in cartoons where they are worn by superheroes, much to children's delight as the mysterious personality behind the mask take on the identity of the portrayed mask. Characters such as Batman, Robin, Spiderman, and Superman are all masked characters.

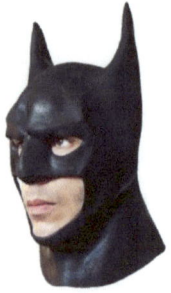 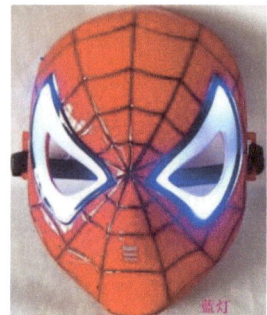

Masks generally cover the whole face, but often it will cover half the face, like a pair of eyeglasses. Half masks are most seen at masquerade parties, carnivals, and Halloween parties.

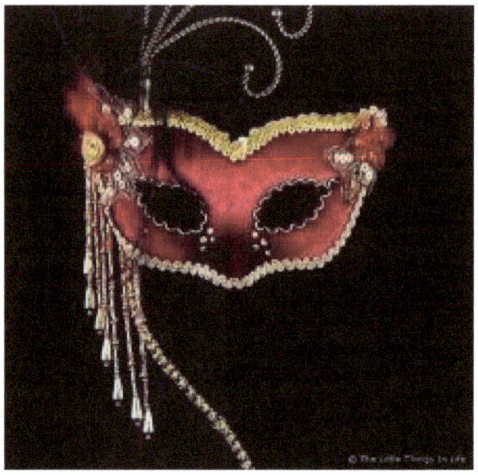

Creating a mask

Mask #1

In creating a mask, a myriad number of materials may be used depending on the type of mask you want to make. Paper, fabric, cardboard, paint, beads, and feathers are just a few of the many things that can be used to create beautiful masks.

The first mask featured here is made from the following:

- Bristol paper,

- glue,

- crayons

- strings

- sprinkles.

These materials are easily accessible.

Method

Fold the Bristol paper in two. Draw a shape on one side of the paper like so:

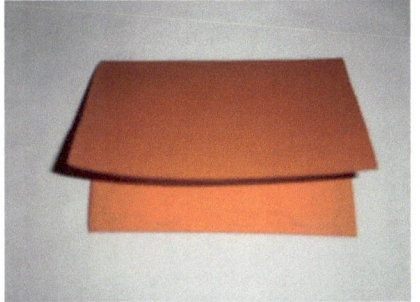

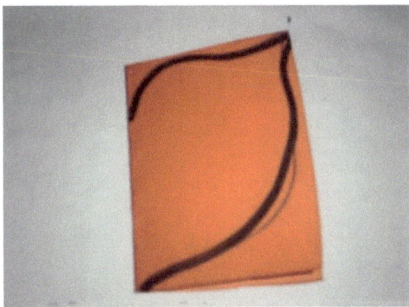

The folded paper.   Half of the mask drawn on one side.

With the paper still folded, cut the along the outlined area. Fold in the area of the eye and make a semi-circular cut. Open the paper to reveal the mask.

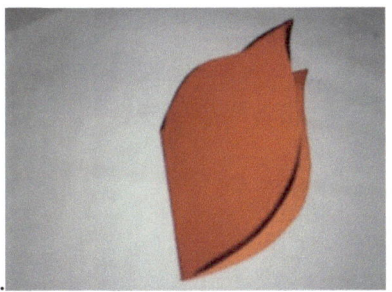

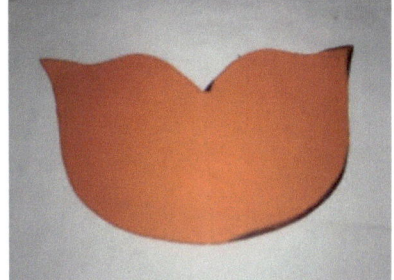

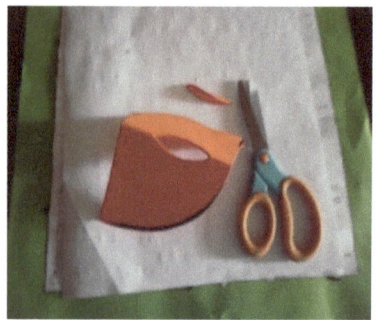
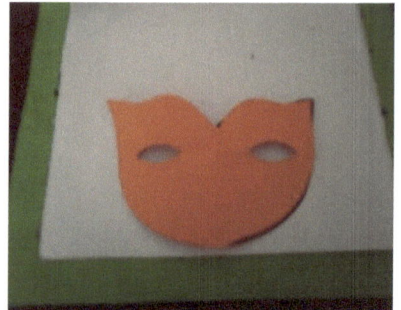

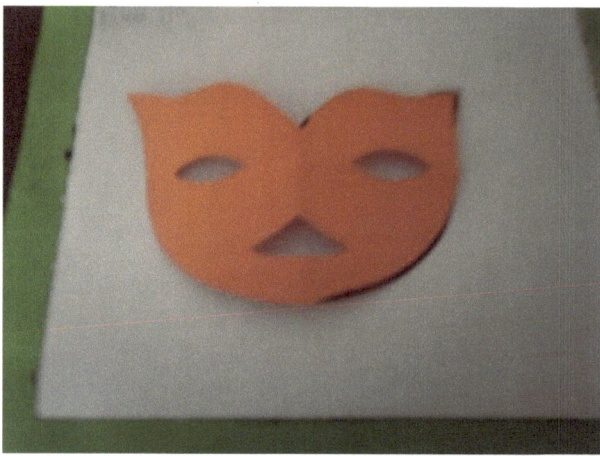

Mask with eyes and mouth cut out

Use crayons and sparkles to create a design on the surface of the mask. Make a hole on each side of the mask and tie a pair of strings to complete the mask.

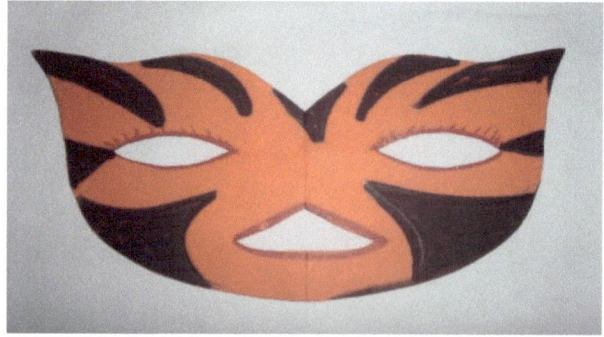

The finished mask

Mask #2

You will need:

- Strips of newspaper

- A balloon

- Glue

- White paint

- Paint (various colours)

- String

The next mask that will be explored will take the shape of the face. The face could actually be used by basing the face with Vaseline and building up the surface with tissue or some other type of paper and glue. In place of a person's face, a blown balloon will be used.

Create a paper pulp by blending strips of newspaper into a blender. Remove the thick pulp from the blender and extract the excess water using a strainer or a mesh. Add a bit of glue to the pulp and put it aside.

Blow up a fairly big balloon and secure the opening by tying it. Glue strips of newspaper, overlapping the pieces until the entire balloon is covered.

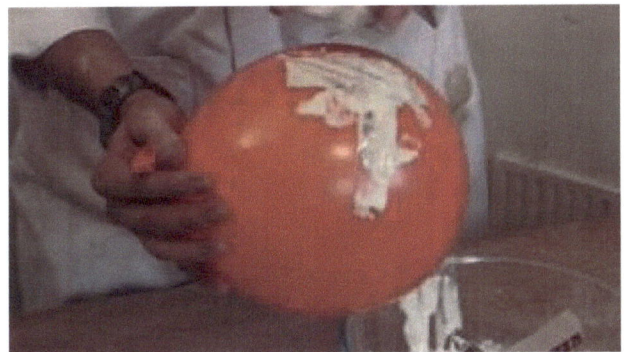

Gently shift and press the pulp onto the balloon form. Add layers of pulp to build up features from the surface.

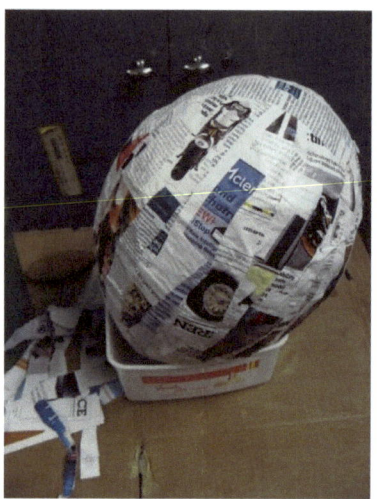

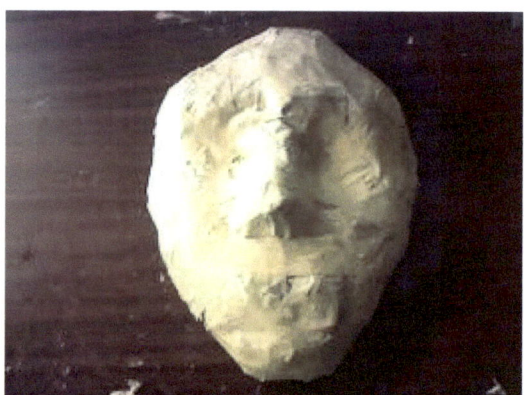

When the desired features are created allow to dry thoroughly, preferably overnight.

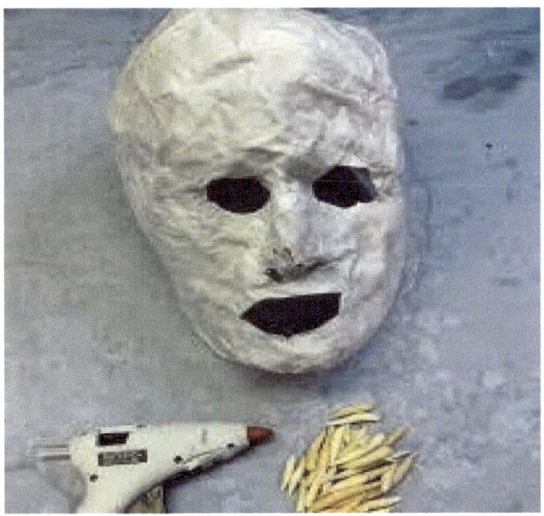

Remove the balloon and use a sharp knife to cut open the eyes and mouth. Decorate using yarn, paint, feathers, beads and other decorative objects of your choice. Tie a string on either sides of the mask to complete the project.

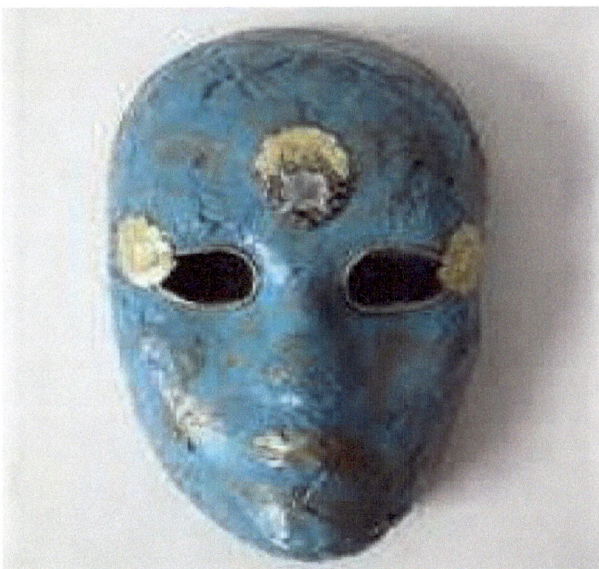

Chapter 11 - Mosaics

Mosaics is an art technique that uses small squares or pieces of stone, glass, tiles, or paper to create images on a surface. These small pieces are fitted together like a puzzle with small spaces between each piece. The small pieces are called tesserae.

Mosaics are generally found on walls or floors, but the technique can be explored on many other types of surfaces including table tops, benches, wooden surfaces, etc.

Mosaics were very common in Rome, Italy, Spain, Portugal and Great Britain.

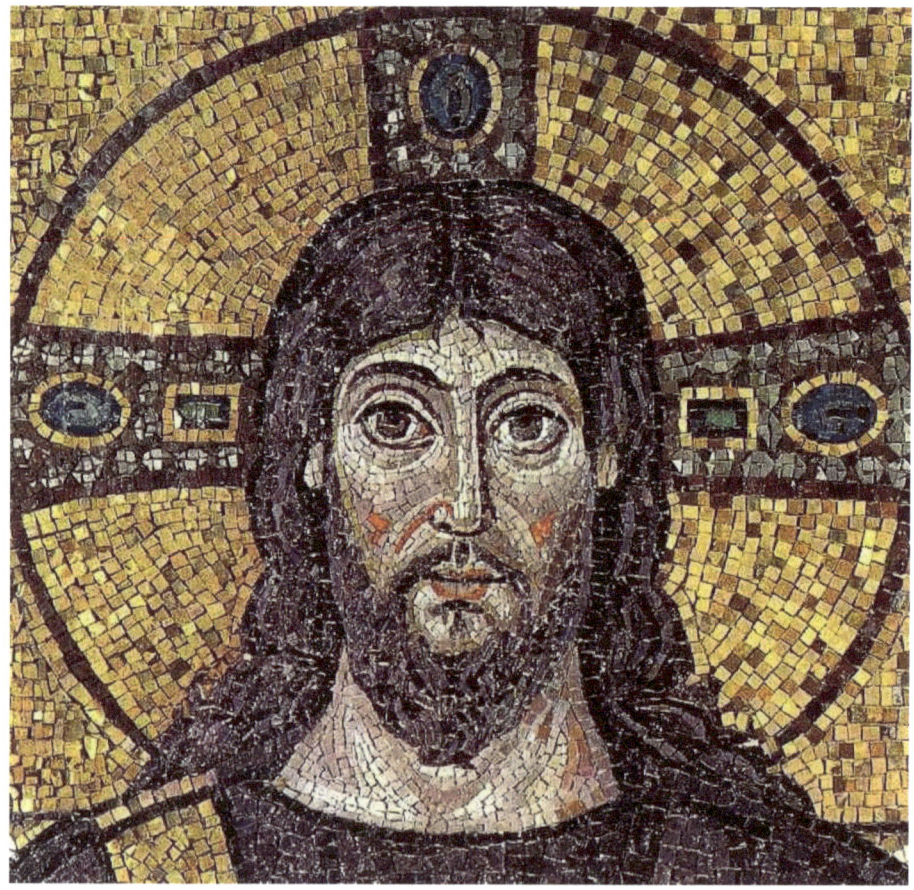

A mosaic of Jesus, done in the 6th century, at the St. Apollinare Nuovo in Europe

For this project we will be using paper instead of tiles, stone or glass.

Materials needed:

- Brightly coloured magazines

- Glue

- Pencil

- Bristol or cartridge paper

- Pencil for sketching design

- Scissors

- Yarn (optional)

Method

Draw a picture of your choice, making it as simple as possible. Decide on the colour scheme of the work.

Tear pages from the magazine and organize pages according to colours, that is; all greens are placed together, all reds together, all blues together, etc.

Cut papers in small squares, keeping the all like colours together. Decide on where the colours will go and begin working from the middle of the design, adding squares and ensuring that there is space between the squares. Upon completion you may decide to outline your work with a bit of yarn.

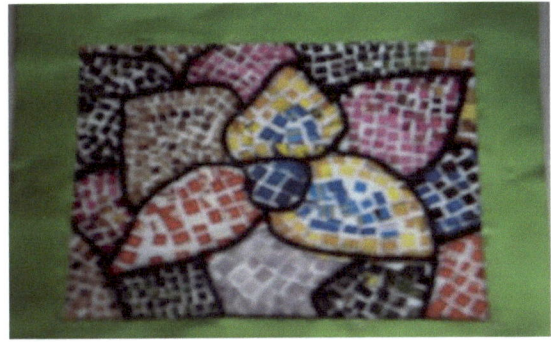

Student's work – Shahila Bennett

Conclusion

These few art projects were designed for children to explore and enjoy. Children must be given the opportunity to exercise their creativity and express themselves. It is only then that they will be rounded and well adjusted individuals as they find their place in their societies and the world.

Author Bio

Evadne Taylor was born in a small rural town of Jamaica. She grew up in the urban areas, however, and studied Visual Arts at the leading Visual and Performing Arts College in the Caribbean. While there, she pursued art education and subsequently became an artist teacher.

For the past 30 years Evadne Taylor has been working with children between the age of 6-12 years where she not only teaches reading, writing and arithmetic, but constantly seeks to engage students in art activities while assisting then to explore their creativity.

Evadne is married with two adult children.

Check out some of the other JD-Biz Publishing books

[Amazing Animal Book Series](#)

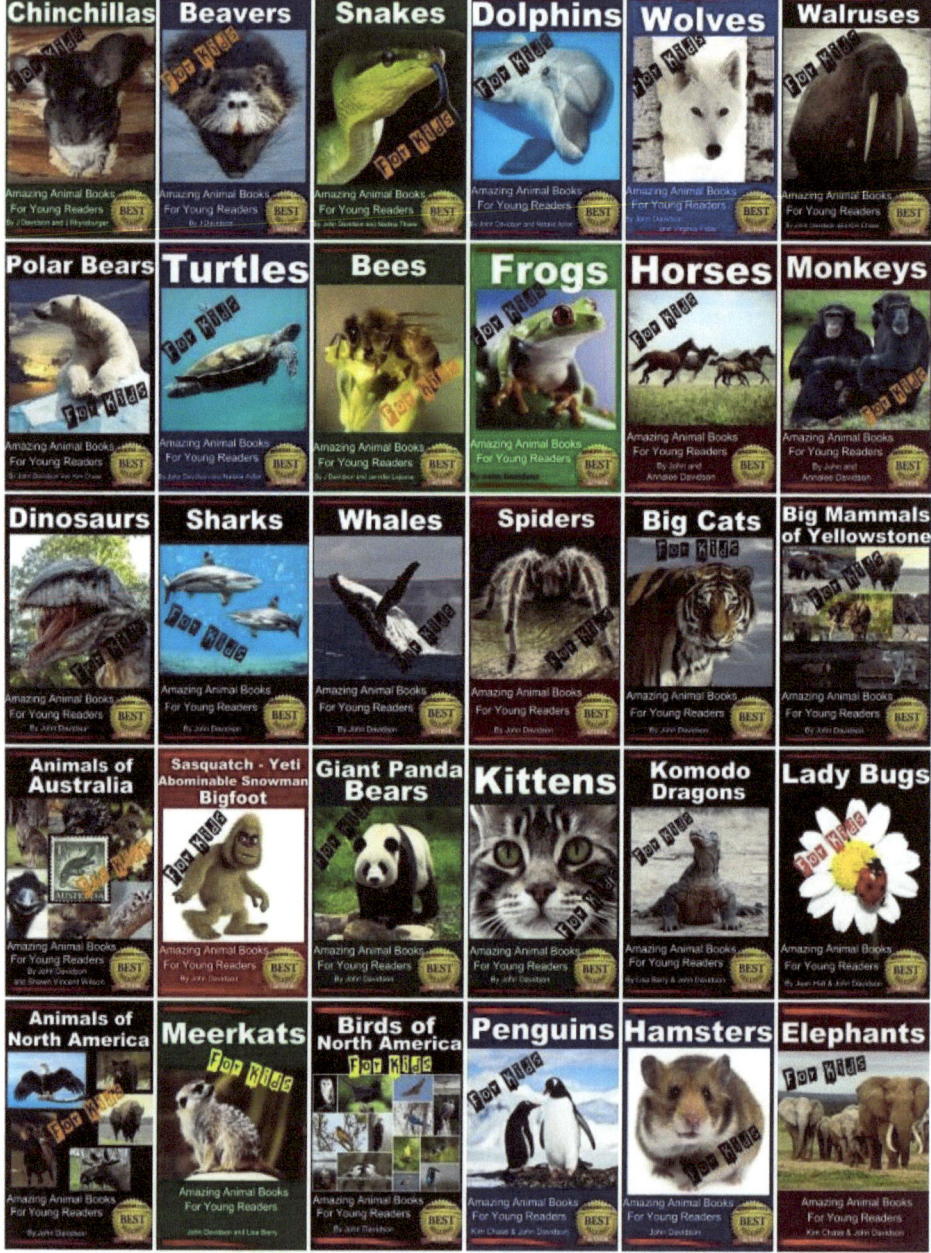

Check out some of the other JD-Biz Publishing books

[Amazing Animal Book Series](#)

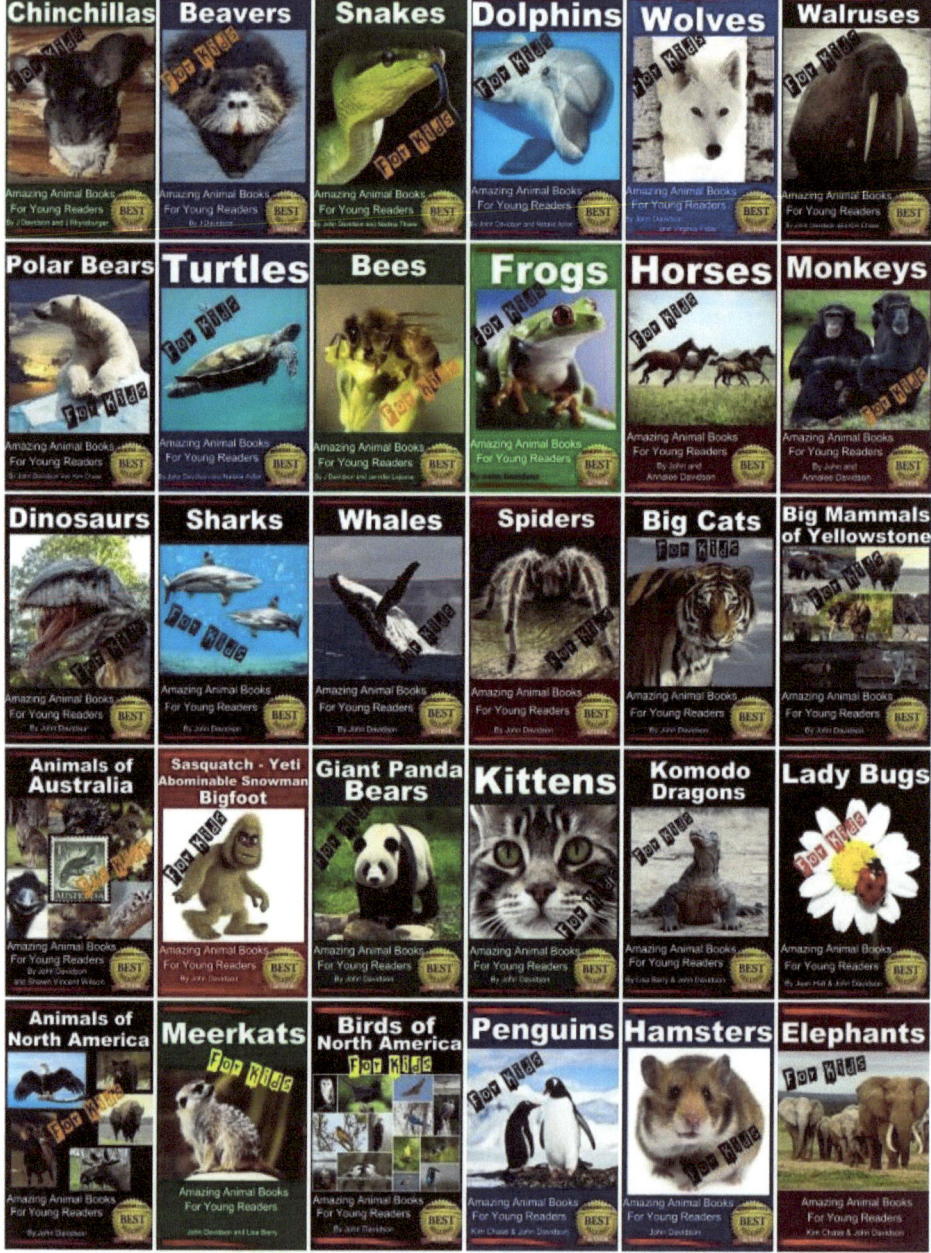

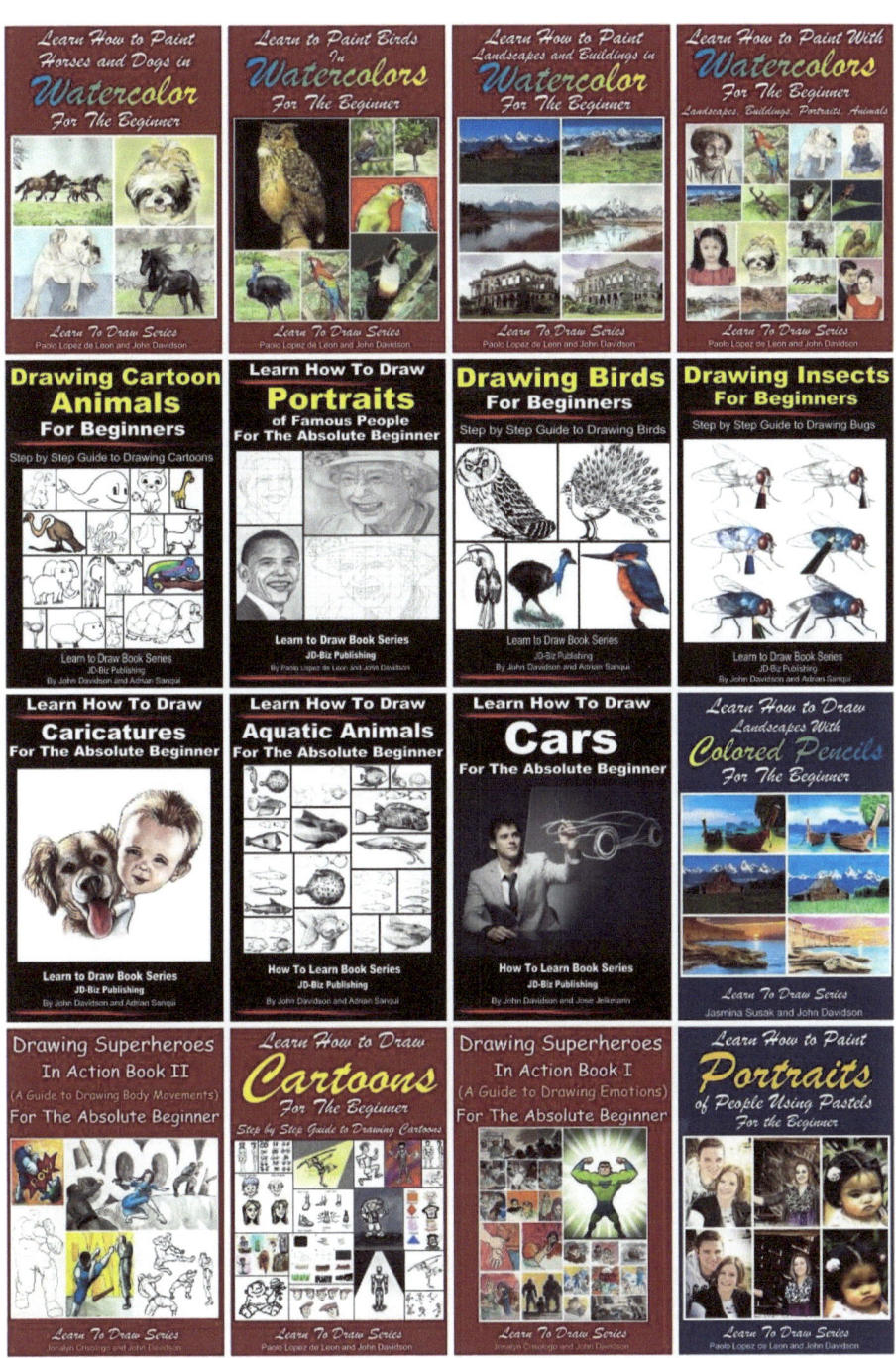

Our books are available at

1. Amazon.com

2. Barnes and Noble

3. Itunes

4. Kobo

5. Smashwords

6. Google Play Books

Publisher

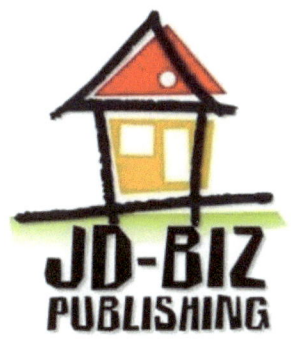

JD-Biz Corp

P O Box 374

Mendon, Utah 84325

http://www.jd-biz.com/

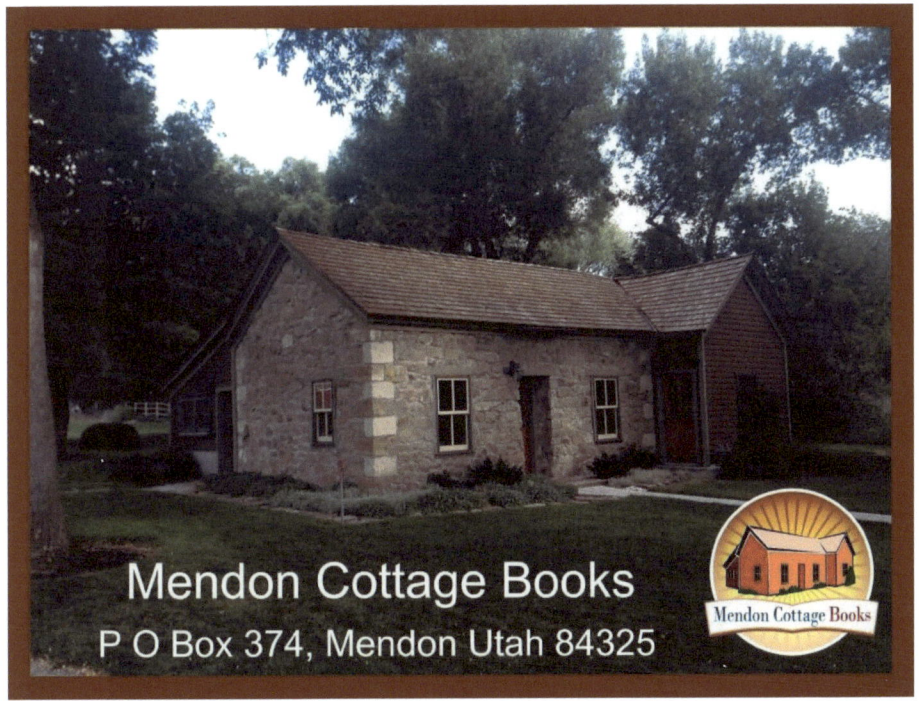

www.ingramcontent.com/pod-product-compliance
Lightning Source LLC
Chambersburg PA
CBHW040922180526
45159CB00002BA/577